how2become

This book is to be returned on or before
the last date stamped below.

WD

Int   d

A de   o
passin   iew

www.How2Become.com

Attend a 1 Day Police Officer Training Course by visiting:

www.PoliceCourse.co.uk

Get more products for passing any selection process at:

www.How2Become.com

Orders: Please contact How2become Ltd, Suite 14, 50 Churchill Square Business Centre, Kings Hill, Kent ME19 4YU.

Please order via the email address info@how2become.co.uk.

ISBN: 9781911259350

First published 2017.

Typeset for How2become Limited by Gemma Butler.

Printed in the UK for How2Become Limited by CMP.

Disclaimer

Every effort has been made to ensure that the information contained within this guide is accurate at the time of publication. How2Become Ltd is not responsible for anyone failing any part of any selection process as a result of the information contained within this guide. How2Become Ltd and their authors cannot accept any responsibility for any errors or omissions within this guide, however caused. No responsibility for loss or damage occasioned by any person acting, or refraining from action, as a result of the material in this publication can be accepted by How2Become Ltd.

The information within this guide does not represent the views of any third party service or organisation.

Contents

Introduction by Richard McMunn   7

My top 10 tips for passing the police officer final interview   11

What to expect at the police officer final interview   19

How to prepare, what to research and what you need to know   23

Police officer final interview questions and answers   37

A few final words   103

Introduction by Richard McMunn

INTRODUCTION BY RICHARD MCMUNN

Dear aspiring police officer,

Before I introduce myself, and more importantly explain how I am going to help you pass the police officer final interview, I want to tell you the difference between a successful candidate, and one that fails.

A successful candidate is one that prepares themselves fully for this final stage of the selection process. A successful candidate is someone who not only believes in their own abilities, but understands the different areas that he or she must concentrate on during their preparation. A successful candidate is someone who has put in many, many hours of preparation, so that they can walk into the interview room knowing they are going to be successful. Conversely, a candidate who fails, is the opposite of all of the above.

I am being genuinely honest when I say to you that the only person in control of whether you pass or fail the final interview, is you. You have control over how much preparation you put into this; you have control over the number of mock interviews that you carry out before the interview day, and you also have control over how you perform at the interview, with regards to interview technique.

Within this guide, I am going to help you prepare to the best of your ability. My advice is for you to read this book at least twice, take notes and also practice everything that you learn. Leave no stone unturned, and you will be successful. Now, allow me to tell you a little bit about myself, and why I'm the right person to teach you about the police officer final interview.

My name is Richard McMunn. I have been helping people like you to obtain the career of their dreams since 2005. More importantly, I have been very successful at it. I measure success by the feedback that my company receives from the many people who manage to obtain their chosen career, after using one of my guides, videos or training courses. I am extremely passionate about helping people pass a particular selection process, and I have taken great care to ensure that the content within this book is both accurate and helpful. I genuinely believe that you will find it a great help, in your preparation for the police officer final interview.

Prior to starting the website **www.How2Become.com**, I worked in the public sector for over 20 years. During that time, I was heavily involved in recruitment, managing assessment centres and also interviewing people like you to join the emergency services. Within this book, I am going to take you on a journey of preparation like no other. By the time you have finished this guide, you will be fully prepared for your interview and more importantly, have the confidence to pass it with flying colours.

Let's get started.

Richard McMunn

My top 10 tips for passing the police officer final interview

My top 10 tips for passing the police officer final interview

Within this early section of the guide, I want to give you my top 10 tips for passing the police officer final interview. I have listed each of the tips in no particular order. Each tip is then immediately followed by a brief narrative, explaining what the tip is, and why I believe it be important. Later on in this guide, we'll cover a number of these tips in even greater detail.

So, without further ado, here are my top 10 tips.

TIP NUMBER 1 – Success is in *your* hands, nobody else's

Before you start preparing for the final interview, remember that the amount of preparation you put into the interview can have an impact on the result. I truly believe that success is in *your* hands, and nobody else's. I have heard some pathetic excuses in my time, for why some people believe they failed the police selection process. The one excuse that I hear time and again is this one:

"I didn't get in because the police are only looking for women, and they don't want white males."

This is complete rubbish. Yes, the police force is actively looking to recruit people from under-represented groups (and rightly so, too), but that does not mean you won't get in because you are *not* from an under-represented group. Just focus on getting the highest scores possible during the final interview, and you will be successful.

Sometimes in life we have to try very hard to get what we want. Sometimes in life we have to keep persevering, even when we fail the first time around. Although the following short story has no relevance to you joining the police force, I wanted to share a personal experience of mine, which I had at the age of 16. This had a significant impact on way that I tackle setbacks in my life.

When I was a teenager (16), I tried to join the Royal Navy. I failed the medical because I was a stone overweight. I can remember leaving the medical at the doctor's surgery, and I was both gutted and humiliated. However, instead of giving up and moaning about my situation, I started running and I also drastically improved my diet. After a month of intense training and improved eating, I applied to join the Royal Navy again; only this time I passed. The reason I failed the first time around was down to me, and conversely the reason why I passed the second time was also down to me. Take responsibility for your own success in life – work hard, continually look for ways to improve and success *will* come your way.

TIP NUMBER 2 – Be someone who embraces change

Working in the public sector is different to how it used to be. When I joined many years ago, we didn't really care much for change. The old adage of *"if it ain't broke don't fix it"* was often heard being said in the workplace. This attitude and approach to working life does not cut it anymore.

The pressure on public sector organisations such as the police force has never been as intense as it is today, and this pressure will only increase as the years go by. As such, the police force needs people who will not only support change, but also embrace it. During your preparation, make sure you are able to provide examples of where you have **supported** and **promoted** change in the workplace. This is very important.

TIP NUMBER 3 – Take responsibility for your own health and fitness

The responsibility to maintain fitness as a police officer rests with you. In my opinion, there is nothing worse than seeing an unfit/obese police officer patrolling the streets. I don't care what anyone says, it just doesn't look right! And for those people who think I am discriminating against people because of their weight, I couldn't care less!

The fact is that a police officer should be able to climb walls and run after/tackle criminals. If they are unable to meet the demands of the job, then unfit police officers could put themselves, their colleagues and the general public in danger. As a police officer you could find yourself in a situation whereby you are required to wear heavy protective equipment whilst tackling mobs during a riot. It is times like this where you will be tested both physically and mentally, and you will need to make sure that you are capable of performing your duties both competently and professionally.

The good news is, you do not need to be mega fit to join the police force. In my view, the fitness standards are set quite low. I would be surprised if you don't get asked a question at the interview that explores what you do in your spare time, and also how you keep yourself physically fit and active. See my sample response to this type of question in the relevant chapter of the guide, for advice on how to answer it.

TIP NUMBER 4 – Be "politically" aware

What do I mean by this? Well, in a nutshell, it means understanding that the police service is exactly that: a service. The police service is not only responsible to the members of the public whom it serves, but it is also responsible to the Government that is in power at that particular time. The Government will generally have a large say in how the police force operates, and on that basis, things can change very quickly from time to time. That is one of the reasons why the police service is keen to employ people who are capable of and willing to accept change. We have all been in jobs before where some of the longest-serving employees have become "dinosaurs". These people are often unhelpful, obstructive and unwilling to accept or embrace change. Don't become one of them, as they are not pleasant to work with. When you join the police force, be willing to embrace change, regardless of how long you have served.

TIP NUMBER 5 – Carry out a mock interview

Trust me, this will really help to boost your confidence before you walk into the interview room. The police officer final interview will be one of the most important interviews you will ever attend. Therefore, you should do all you can to be at your peak on the day. One of the best tips I can give you is to carry out at least one mock interview before your big day (preferably three or four!). A mock interview involves asking a friend or relative to sit down in front of you and ask you all of the questions contained within this guide. The final interview will probably last for approximately 60 minutes; therefore, you have to be capable of doing the majority of talking for that length of time. Don't let the first time that you answer the questions I have provided within this guide be at the actual interview itself. You want your answers to the questions to flow, and the only way you will achieve this is by practicing your answers before the real thing.

TIP NUMBER 6 – Provide lots of evidence when answering the interview questions

Evidence, evidence, evidence. If you have got this far in the selection process, you will have already demonstrated your ability to provide answers to competency-based interview questions at the assessment centre interview. Don't be fooled into thinking you won't need to provide further evidence during the final interview, because you will. Make sure you have sufficient evidence to offer the panel, for all of the core competencies that are required of the role of police officer. In addition to this, and as part of your study, make sure you prepare answers to the "additional" interview questions, which I have included towards the end of this guide. There are a number of situational questions contained within that particular part. Finally, when answering situational interview questions, use the STAR technique for structuring your responses:

Situation – What was the situation you were in?

Task – What was the task that you and others had to carry out, and what difficulties did you have to overcome along the way?

Action – What action did you and others take whilst carrying out the task? (Tip: when responding to "team-related" situational interview questions, refer to the team as "we", as opposed to "I".

Result – What was the result following yours and the team's actions?

Finally, at the end of your response, tell the interview panel what you **LEARNT** from the process and what, if anything, you would do differently next time.

TIP NUMBER 7 – Have a thorough understanding of the role of a police officer, and also the role of the police force

You don't need me to tell you that you should have a thorough understanding of the role of a police officer, and also the role of the police force, before you attend your interview. However, you would be amazed at how many people get caught out by simple questions such as:

Q. Tell me what you would expect to be doing on a day-to-day basis as a police officer?

And

Q. What is the primary role of the police force and what, exactly, are our objectives?

Whilst I will go into more detail during tip number 10 about not getting caught out by easy questions, do make sure you know exactly what the role of a police officer and the police force is.

TIP NUMBER 8 – Carry on studying the core competencies

As boring as they might seem, the core competencies should still form an integral part of your study whilst preparing for the police officer final interview. Although you will have already demonstrated your ability to match these during the assessment centre interview, do make sure you carry on studying them and, more importantly, be able to provide sufficient evidence of how you match each and every one.

TIP NUMBER 9 – Be prepared to ask the panel two questions at the end of the interview

At the end of the interview, it is good practice to ask a couple of questions, if invited to do so. At the end of the sample interview questions and answers section of this guide, I have provided two sample questions that you might consider asking. However, I also think it's good practice to come up with a couple of your own. Just make sure that, whatever questions you do ask, they are intelligent and they are not designed to catch the interview panel out or make you look clever.

TIP NUMBER 10 – Don't get caught out at the start of the interview!

More often than not, it can be the "easy" questions that we find the hardest to answer. Questions such as *'Why do you want to be a police officer?'* and *'What areas do you most need to improve on?'* can often catch us off guard. Therefore, make sure you prepare just as much for the easy questions as for the harder situational-type questions. To help you prepare in this area, here are some tips:

- Consider what you do well (what are you good at?);

- Consider which areas you need to develop or which areas do you need to work on. (In particular, are there any aspects of the initial recruit training course you might find difficult or challenging?);

- Assess your strengths and development areas (what are you doing to improve on your development areas, especially in your current job?);

- Consider what is important to you;

- Consider what you find challenging;

- Review how others may perceive you (be prepared to answer truthfully about how other people perceive you and take steps to improve in areas that need development. Remember, police officers should act with integrity and honesty at all times).

Now let's move on to the next section of the guide which is titled "What to expect at the police officer final interview".

What to expect at the police officer final interview

Chapter 1 – What to expect at the police officer final interview

In a nutshell, here's what to expect at the interview:

- The final interview will normally be carried out at the police force headquarters or training establishment;

- There is no "formal" structure to the interview and each police force is permitted to carry out the interview under their own terms and format;

- The final interview is used to whittle down the numbers of police officers that they require for that particular recruitment intake;

- There will be 2-3 people on the interview panel;

- One or two members of the interview panel will be serving police officers (senior level);

- One member of the panel will be a member of the Human Resources (HR) department;

- Depending on how long your answers to the questions are, the interview will usually last for between 45-60 minutes;

The above information will give you a brief introduction as to what to expect during the police officer final interview. During the interview you will be assessed against a number different areas, including:

- Your motivations for wanting to become a police officer;

- Your knowledge of the role;

- What you know about the constabulary that you are applying to join;

- Your knowledge and understanding of the police officer core competencies (yes, you could get asked more competency-based questions!);

- What you have been doing in order to prepare for the interview and the role of a police officer, if successful;

- Information relating to your completed application form (make sure you revisit this prior to the interview);

- What you would do and how you would react in certain situations;

- What evidence you can provide to back up your claim that you can meet the competencies;

- What you do in your spare time;

- Past achievements and work experience;

- Your strengths and weaknesses;

- The type of person you are, including your character and level of honesty and integrity;

- How flexible (work-related) you are as a person;

- What your friends and family think of you joining the police force, and how much they support you;

- Your communication skills during the interview;

- Your interview technique and how you present yourself to the panel.

You may also get asked a question based on your knowledge and awareness of what is happening to the police service, both locally and nationally (police news and developments). The above list is not exhaustive, and you could get asked questions based on additional areas too. The key to your success at the final interview is to prepare as fully as possible. By preparing fully, you will ensure your confidence levels are high, and that you will be capable of answering the questions presented to you.

So, now that we know a little bit more about the interview and how we will be assessed, let's move on to the next section. Here, I will teach you how to prepare, what to research and what you need to know.

How to prepare, what to research and what you need to know

Chapter 2 – How to prepare, what to research and what you need to know

In this section of the guide, we are going to move on to the next stage of your development. Here, I will explain how you can prepare effectively for your interview, and also the different areas that you will need to research.

In order to achieve this, we need to look at the following key areas:

- Interview technique;

- Research areas.

Of course, the amount of time that you have to prepare for your interview will very much depend on how many days or weeks there are until your interview. Regardless of how much time you have left before your interview, please do make sure you put the hours in. The more time you dedicate to your preparation, the higher your chances of success will be.

Interview technique

Although some people reading this section will think that I cannot teach them anything new regarding "interview technique", I would plead with them to stick with me and thoroughly read this section. Interview technique, or more importantly how you present yourself visually and verbally at the interview, is just as important as how you respond to the questions.

First and foremost, always remember that you are attempting to join a "public service", which prides itself on honesty, integrity and very high standards. Of course, the police service does not always get things right, but they are constantly trying to, and as such, they need to employ people within their organisation who aspire to be the best that they can possibly be. On that basis, during the interview, you need to demonstrate that you can act as a positive **role model** for the police, and provide proof that you will not let them down.

The police force requires its officers to wear a uniform. That uniform must be worn with pride, and it is your responsibility to make sure that it is clean, pressed and worn to the standards expected of the force at all times.

Wearing a smart, formal outfit to the interview, will go a long way to demonstrating to the panel you are capable of looking after yourself. Trust me, after interviewing literally hundreds of people over the years for various jobs, including jobs in the emergency services, it never ceases to amaze me how some people are incapable of wearing the correct attire to an interview. I don't care what anyone says, if you turn up to an interview scruffily dressed, or your shoes are not clean, no amount of "great responses" to the interview questions will land you the job.

So, here are a few important guidelines to follow:

1. Wear a smart suit or formal outfit to the interview. You do not need to go out and buy a new or expensive suit for your interview, but do make sure that what you wear is clean, pressed and representative of the appearance you want to portray to the panel.

2. Avoid wearing bright coloured clothes. By this, I mean cartoon-blazoned ties, Mickey Mouse socks or even red shoes. Just stick to conservative colours and you will be fine. Try to **stand out for the right reasons** and not for the clothes you wear.

3. When we meet someone for the first time, we form a view or opinion of them within the first seven seconds. You can start to **create a positive impression** of yourself even before you walk into the interview room. When you arrive at the location at which the interview is going to take place, you will probably be asked to wait in the reception area. Be polite to the reception staff upon arrival, and sit down in the waiting area chair sat upright, as you would do whilst sat in the interview chair. When you are eventually asked to go to the interview room, knock on the door confidently and don't enter until invited to do so. When you do walk into the interview room, immediately introduce yourself by standing upright and saying:

"Good morning/afternoon, my name is XXXXX, pleased to meet you."

Then, walk over to the interview chair and do not sit down until invited to do so.

Once sat down in the interview chair, sit upright with your hands resting on your knees, palms faced down. Don't cross your legs and do not slouch at any time during the interview.

4. Naturally, you are going to be nervous during the interview; this is to be expected. However, it is important to be **confident in your own abilities** during the interview and you should also smile and engage in a positive manner with the interviewers.

5. Listen carefully to what each person on the interview panel says. You can demonstrate "effective listening skills" whilst each member of the panel is talking, simply by nodding and using soft facial expressions. All of this should come naturally, so make sure you practice this during your mock interviews (more on these later). One great tip that I want to give you, is to practice responding to the interview questions whilst sitting in front of a mirror. Try answering the questions "Tell me about yourself?" whilst sitting in front of a mirror, and see how you get on. This is likely to be one of the first questions the panel will ask you, so it would be good to have a response ready and prepared before your actual interview. By responding to this question in the mirror, you will get a good idea of how you will come across and look to the interview panel.

6. Remember that you are being assessed against your **potential to be a police officer**. You do not need to be the finished article at the interview; however, you do need to demonstrate that you have all the qualities and attributes required to become a competent officer. You must ensure you know the core competencies inside out before you attend the final interview. Do not make the mistake that some people do, whereby they don't bother learning or re-reading the core competencies after the assessment centre interview, simply because they think they have passed that particular stage and it won't get assessed again. You will more than likely be asked questions during the final interview on how you meet the core competencies, so make sure you know these in detail, and more importantly, be capable of providing "evidence" of where you meet and match every single one of them.

7. Good interview technique also means knowing what **questions you are going to ask** at the end of the interview. I get asked time and again whether someone should bother to ask questions at the end of the interview. Let me answer it like this – If you don't have any questions to ask, and the panel have told you everything you wanted to know during the interview, don't waste their time asking irrelevant questions. It is perfectly OK to just say something like:

"To be honest, you have answered everything I wanted to know during the interview and on that basis, I do not have any questions, thank you."

However, if you do want to ask questions at the end, have two (or three at the absolute most) already prepared. Here are examples of questions you could ask the panel at the end of the interview:

Q1. *During my study whilst preparing for selection process, I was studying your website and I noticed you have managed to significantly reduce theft from cars over the last 12 months due to your proactive work with other agencies. I wondered whether the good practices you have been deploying to reduce this type of crime gets shared with other police forces across the country, so that they can use your methods in order to reduce crime in their area?*

The above question demonstrates that you have spent time studying their website in detail, whilst also showing a desire to understand how the police reduces crime on a national level. This is a very good question to ask! OK, here's another one:

Q2. *Whilst I am waiting to find out whether or not I have been successful, can you recommend any websites or further literature I could study to learn more about the police force?*

The above question demonstrates that you are *hungry* to learn more about the police force and the good work they carry out.

Personally, I think two questions to ask at the end of the interview is sufficient. Providing the questions you ask are intelligent, and they put you across in a positive light, two will be fine.

I am sure you don't really need me to tell you these; however, the following are a list of questions that I recommend you **do not** ask the panel at the end of your interview:

Q. How long is the training course to become a police officer? (You should already know this!)

Q. I have some holiday booked in a few weeks' time. Could this be an issue if I am successful? (You are effectively saying here that your holiday is more important than your police officer training.)

Q. How much leave will I get per year? (Not a great question to ask,

I'm sure you will agree. You should already know how much leave an officer gets).

So, to summarise, it is perfectly fine to ask a couple of questions at the end of the interview, but do make sure they are intelligent questions and not ones that either catch the panel out, or put you in a negative light.

8. Final impressions are just as important as first impressions. What do I mean by this? Well, to put it in simple terms, what you *do* and *say* at the end of the police officer final interview can have an impact on how you will be assessed. There is a strong chance that the interview panel will spend a short period of time assessing you and discussing your performance, immediately following the interview. I am a strong believer that saying a genuine, honest and **positive statement** at the end of an interview can help lift your scores. If I were attending the final interview right now, I would say the following at the end, just before I got up to leave:

> *"I would just like to say thank you for interviewing me today, and I have thoroughly enjoyed the experience of going through the selection process. If I am successful, I promise you that I will work hard to not only uphold the values and standards that the police force expects of its officers, but I will also continue to work hard throughout my career to deliver a high standard of service to the public. Thank you."*

The above statement, providing you do actually mean it and you say it with conviction, will be the last thing the panel remembers you for when you walk out of the interview door. If they are then going to assess your performance once you leave the room, this can only be a positive thing.

TOP TIP: I strongly believe that you can drastically increase your chances of passing the police officer final interview if you carry out at least one mock interview before you attend the real thing. A mock interview is where you ask a friend or relative to sit down, and ask you all of the interview questions contained within this guide. This will give you the opportunity to try out your responses in a "safe" environment; one where it is OK to make mistakes. The first time you answer the questions contained within this guide should not be at the real interview! Try out at least one mock interview (preferably three or four) and see how you get on.

Research areas

Before we move onto the all-important sample interview questions and answers, we need to cover the areas you must research during your preparation for the final interview.

Now, although this section is relatively comprehensive, I fully understand that some of you reading this will not have long to prepare for your police final interview. On that basis, if you only have a couple of days until your interview, skip this section and study the sample interview questions that I have provided within the next chapter. You can then start to work on your proposed responses to the questions supplied, in the time you have available. Conversely, if you have a couple of weeks or even longer before your interview, study this section carefully, take notes and then start researching the different areas I have recommended within the content.

To make the section easier for you to read, I have provided a list of each particular research area, including a brief explanation of each one below it.

RESEARCH AREA #1 – CORE COMPETENCIES

Yes, I know, these are boring! However, they form an important part of your preparation, because the competencies themselves are the blueprint for the role of a police officer. It is therefore understandable that the police force you are applying to join want to know that you have the experience and evidence to match each and every one of them.

When researching and learning the core competencies, follow this advice:

- Read the core competencies, and be able to explain what each one is, if asked. For example, an interview question might be **"can you tell me what the core competency of working with others is, and also provide me with an example of when you have worked as part of a team to achieve an important task?"** If you have the time, write down each competency on a flip-card, and carry them around with you. Then, when you have a spare few minutes during the day, get the flip-cards out and learn them.

- Be able to provide evidence of where you match each and every one of the core competencies. If you are at the final interview stage of the selection process, then you will have already done this during the assessment centre interview; therefore, you shouldn't have much problem in doing this for each competency being assessed. When providing evidence, structure your responses in this manner:

  SITUATION: What was the situation you were in?

  TASK: What did you have to do and why?

  ACTION: What action did you and others take?

  RESULT: What was the outcome/result of yours and others actions?

- Another important tip that I can give you when trying to match the core competencies, is to use keywords from the competency and use them in your response to the questions. For example, whilst responding to questions that require you to demonstrate **openness to change**, the following phrases might help to improve your score:

  - I was **positive about the change** at all times.

  - I **adapted quickly** to the new way of working whilst **embracing** the change positively.

  - I worked hard and put in **extra effort** to ensure the changes worked for the organisation.

  - In order to help the changes work for the organisation, I **adopted a flexible working attitude**.

  - As a team, we discussed **alternative ways** to make the required changes to working-practices a success.

  - During the process of change, I made a number of suggestions to my line manager that I felt could **support and improve** the transition.

  - I took an **innovative approach** to **solving the problems** we were faced with by doing XYZ.

RESEARCH AREA #2 – THE ROLE OF A POLICE OFFICER

I'd be rather surprised if this question did not appear at some stage of the final interview. Most people going through the selection process *think* that they know what the role of a police officer involves, but in actual fact only a small percentage of them *actually* know. Here is a list of the more prominent areas of the role of a police officer:

- Work to protect members of society from the effects of violence and crime;

- Patrol the streets, in order to provide a reassuring presence in the local community;

- Provide help and support to both victims of crime and also those who have witnessed crimes, or who are affected by it;

- Carry out investigations of crimes;

- Liaise with external agencies/departments in order to solve crime, prevent it and also educate the public;

- Respond to 999 calls and also general non-emergency calls from the public for assistance;

- Record and investigate crime and non-crime issues, including taking details notes of each situation you encounter;

- Work towards securing long-term resolutions to new and on-going community problems;

- Undertake mobile and foot patrol, seeking to reassure the public and proactively work towards the prevention and detection of offences;

- Attend and investigate traffic collisions, working with other agencies to improve road safety;

- Interview suspects, witnesses and victims, establishing facts and compiling case files for prosecution and other further action;

- Arrest and detain suspected persons, gathering evidence to enable the fair and just prosecution of offenders.

The above list is not exhaustive. On that basis, I recommend that you study the website of the police force you are applying to join, to see what they write about the role of a police officer in their particular area/region.

RESEARCH AREA #3 - THE POLICE FORCE YOU ARE APPLYING TO JOIN

This is another key area of research. There are many different areas of the police force. In my opinion, you should try your best to research as many of these as you can. They include:

- The geographical area of the police force.

- Facts and figures relating to the county/region, including how many people the police force protects (total number of people living in the county), the names of the districts, towns and or parish councils (if applicable).

- The senior management team (names and ranks), including the police and crime commissioner.

- The latest news and development stories.

- The key issues effecting the community/county.

- Statistics relating to crime in the county/region.

- What the police force is proactively doing to combat crime and also reduce it.

- The locations of all the police stations within the county, plus the location of the training centre and the force headquarters.

- The principles of policing. (NOTE: These might be included on the force's website. See the sample interview questions and answers section for a response to this question).

- The police force's code of ethics. (NOTE: Again this might be included on the force's website. See the sample interview questions and answers section for a response to this question).

- The police force's equality objectives (if applicable).

- How the police force supports its staff (NOTE: This, if applicable to your chosen force, can usually be found on their website).

Once again, the above list is not exhaustive. Whilst carrying out your research, and in particular studying the force's website, you may find different areas you could get asked questions on.

RESEARCH AREA #4 – PREPARING RESPONSES TO INTERVIEW QUESTIONS BASED ON WHAT YOU WOULD DO IN CERTAIN SITUATIONS

No amount of preparation can prepare you "fully" for every eventuality, with regards to situational interview questions. Having said that, I do feel strongly that you can be as prepared as possible, providing you follow a few simple guidelines which I have detailed within this research area. Before I get into them, allow me to explain what a "situational" interview question is:

Police officers are presented with difficult and challenging situations in every day of their working life. Their actions, and more importantly the decisions they make when presented with these challenging situations, can have a profound effect on the level of service that the force provides. It also impacts on the way in which the general public perceives the police. Therefore, it is perfectly reasonable to expect that the interview panel will ask you at least one question that explores what you think you might do in a given situation.

In order to allow me to explain this further, take a look at the following sample situational interview question and then decide how you might react in the situation.

Q. You are a serving police officer, and you are on foot patrol in the local town centre on a busy Friday night. The time is 11pm, and a member of public runs up to you and tells you a fight has just started in the pub opposite. You look over to the pub and you can see the fight has already spilled out into the road. From what you can see, there appears to be a group of at least ten men fighting. What would you do?

So, as you can see, this type of question has the potential to throw you, if you are unprepared. Of course, the interview panel will not expect you to know the exact "text book" answer to this type of question, but your response will give them a fairly good idea as to the thought process that you would deploy when presented with difficult and challenging situations. To help you understand how to prepare for this type of interview question, consider the following points:

- Regardless of the situation you are presented with, it is vital you stay calm and in control.

- Always remember to state that you would follow your training in any given situation, and also follow the operational procedures employed by the force that you are applying to join.

- Police officers need to be confident and resilient, and you will need to state that you would take some course of action, as opposed to just standing back and seeing how the situation unfolds.

- Although it is not reasonable to expect you to understand the process of "risk assessment" before you join the police, my advice is to understand what a risk assessment is, and how it is used by the police in this type of situation. (NOTE: See my note below that explains in brief what a risk assessment is.)

- As a serving police officer, you would have access to additional resources, if required. In this type of situation, it is clear that you will need assistance/back-up, and therefore this is one of the first things you would request.

NOTE: A risk assessment is a systematic process of evaluating the potential risks that may be involved in a project, activity, situation or undertaking. With regards to the situation presented in the interview question above, it is clear the risks presented are: the number of people involved, the danger presented to the public, the fact that you are on your own and also the fact that violence is involved. These factors will determine the course of action that you would be likely to take in this situation.

You can read a sample response to this interview question in the **sample interview questions and answers** section of the guide.

RESEARCH AREA #5 – MISCELLANEOUS

Here, I have included a miscellaneous section, simply because the final areas of research that I want you to concentrate on, do not fit into any of the other four categories. The areas of research, or should I say preparation, include:

- Questions relating to your integrity and character
- Your motivations for joining the police force
- What you have been doing to prepare for the role of a police officer
- How flexible you are (I don't mean stretching!)
- What you understand about the training you will go through, and the areas that you might struggle with
- What you do in your spare time
- What your friends and family think of you wanting to join the police force
- How you keep yourself physically (and mentally) fit

As you can see from the areas above, you can't really "research" them; however, you can prepare your responses to these types of questions. I have included a series of sample questions and answers in the next section to assist you.

So, plenty of research and preparation areas for you to be getting on with there. I will now dedicate an entire section of this guide to sample interview questions and answers. I am guessing that most of you reading this guide will find these to be quite helpful during your preparation.

Police officer final interview questions and answers

Police officer final interview questions and answers

In this section of the guide, I will provide you with a list of sample final interview questions and answers. The questions I provide are certainly not guaranteed to appear at your own interview; however, if you use these questions in addition to your own research, I feel you will be as fully prepared as possible.

It is also very important for me to stress that the sample responses I provide **are not to be copied or used directly at your own interview.** By all means take ideas and suggestions from the responses that I have provided, but do make sure that any responses you give at your police officer final interview are based on your own personal and professional experiences.

You should also be aware that, although I have provided you with 30 sample interview questions and answers, the likelihood is that you will not get asked anywhere near that number. However, your job whilst preparing for the interview is to have answers for any question that comes your way.

Following each interview question and sample response, I have provided you with a blank page and template for you to write your own personal and individual response.

SAMPLE INTERVIEW QUESTION 1

Q. Tell me about yourself and what qualities you believe you have, that will be relevant to the role of a police officer.

A. To begin with, I am a hard-working, committed and highly-motivated person who prides himself on the ability to continually learn and develop new skills. I am 31 years old, and I currently work as a customer services manager for a transportation company. Prior to taking up this role approximately ten years ago, I spent five years working as a front-line soldier in the Army. In addition to being a family person, I also have my own hobbies and interests, which include team sports such as football and also playing the guitar in a local band.

I am a loyal person, who has a strong track record at work for being reliable, flexible and customer-focused. My annual appraisals are consistently to a high standard and I am always willing to learn new skills. Before applying for this job, I studied the role of a police officer and also the role of the police service in depth, to make sure I was able to meet the requirements of the role. Having been working for my current employer for almost ten years now, I wanted to make sure that I had the potential to become a competent police officer before applying. Job stability is important to me and my family. If successful, I plan to stay in the police force for many years.

Finally, I believe that the additional qualities I possess would benefit the role of a police officer. These include being physically and mentally fit, organisationally and politically aware, determined, reliable, an excellent team player, organised, committed, capable of acting as a positive role model for the police force and being fully open to change.

SAMPLE INTERVIEW QUESTION 1 TEMPLATE

Q. **Tell me about yourself and what qualities you believe you have, that will be relevant to the role of a police officer.**

SAMPLE INTERVIEW QUESTION 2

Q. Why do you want to become a police officer and what made you decide to apply?

A. I have wanted to become a police officer for almost four years now, and I can distinctly remember the time I decided this would be the job for me. I was walking through my local high street on my way to the gym on an early Saturday morning, when I noticed two police officers dealing with an aggressive and verbally abusive young man who, from what I understood later on, had been caught shoplifting from the newsagents in the high street. Whilst walking past, I stopped a few yards on, to see how the police officers would handle the situation. The two police officers remained totally calm and in control of the situation, despite the abuse being directed at them by the man. Their body language was non-confrontational, and they appeared to be using well-thought out techniques to get him to calm down. Once the man had calmed down, the officers arrested him and took him away in their police car. From that point on I wanted to learn more about the role of a police officer. I felt that, due to my previous experiences in the Armed Forces and also my natural abilities, I had what it takes to become a competent police officer. I studied your website and also learnt all about the core competencies of the role. I then realised that I had the potential to become a police officer, and I have been waiting to apply ever since. In addition to this, I have lived in the local community for virtually all my life, and I feel proud that we live in a society that is, overall, safe and a great place to live. I understand a large part of the role of being a police officer is reactive, but I would also be interested in working on the proactive and educational side of the job, whereby you get to educate the public to help keep them safe and also prevent crime from happening in the first place. Finally, whilst I very much like my current job, and feel a debt of gratitude to my employer, I am very much ready for a new challenge and the next stage of my career. I believe I would be an excellent police officer if successful, and can assure you I would work hard to uphold the principles and the values the force expects from its employees.

SAMPLE INTERVIEW QUESTION 2 TEMPLATE

Q. Why do you want to become a police officer and what made you decide to apply?

SAMPLE INTERVIEW QUESTION 3

Q. What are the nine principles of policing, and why do you think we have them?

A. The nine principles of policing are accountability, honesty, fairness, integrity, leadership, objectivity, openness, respect and selflessness. I believe the principles are there to act as the foundations for the role of a police officer. Without the principles, the police force would not be able to provide the high level of service it does. I believe that the nine principles would be important for me to learn, absorb, understand and abide by, throughout the duration of my career as a police officer.

Accountability ensures that things get done, and that they get done to a high standard. The general public expects the police force to be open, honest and transparent, and to always act with the highest levels of integrity at all times. Without leadership or direction, the police force would not have the reputation around the world that it currently has. Selflessness means having more concern about the needs and wishes of others than with one's own, and finally, respect is absolutely vital, especially as we live in an extremely diverse community. Respect is a basic human right and it is important we all respect each other at work and in society, regardless of race, gender, sexual orientation, age or religion.

SAMPLE INTERVIEW QUESTION 3 TEMPLATE

Q. What are the nine principles of policing, and why do you think we have them?

SAMPLE INTERVIEW QUESTION 4

Q. Tell me what work you have done during your preparation for applying to become a police officer?

A. I have carried out a huge amount of work, research and personal development on my journey to being here today. To begin with, I studied the role of a police officer, especially with regards to the core competencies. I wanted to make sure that I could meet the requirements of the role, so I asked myself whether I had sufficient evidence and experience to match each and every one of the core competencies. Once I was certain that I had the experience in life, I started to find out more about the work the police carry out, both on a local and national level. I have studied your website in detail, and learnt as much as I possibly could about how you tackle crime, deal with the effects of it and also how you use statistics to drive down increasing crime trends in specific areas. I have also briefly read some of the important policing policies you employ, such as the Operations and Partnership policy, the Human Resources policy and also the Professional Standards policy. Whilst I admit I did not read these in great detail, I wanted to make sure that I was prepared as possible for my interview today. In addition to reading and researching, I went along to my local police station to try and find out a bit more about the job, and the expectations that the public have from the police. The police officer I spoke to was understandably very busy, but she did give me fifteen minutes of her time, whereby she explained what the job involved, what it was like working shifts and also the good points and challenging points about the job. After speaking with her, I felt I had a better understanding of the role and it only made me want to apply even more. Finally, although I believe I am relatively fit, I started attending the gymnasium more to build up my physical strength and stamina. I also worked hard at increasing my times during the bleep test, and I can now get to level twelve since starting my application to join the police. I am very determined to become a police officer, and on that basis I have carried out lots of research to find out as much as I could about the role.

SAMPLE INTERVIEW QUESTION 4 TEMPLATE

Q. Tell me what work you have done during your preparation for applying to become a police officer?

SAMPLE INTERVIEW QUESTION 5

Q. If you witnessed a member of your team at work being verbally abused, what would you do?

A. First and foremost, I would intervene and stop it. Any type of abuse, both physical or verbal should not be tolerated either in society or in the workplace. Everybody should feel safe at work and I believe I would have a responsibility as an employee to intervene. Having said that, I would always make sure I followed the organisation's policy on bullying and harassment, and also follow the necessary reporting procedures required of me when dealing with such a situation. I would always remain calm and non-confrontational in a situation like this, and I would also take the opportunity to educate the offender on why their behaviour was not acceptable. I would also speak to the person who was being verbally abused, to offer my support and to be on hand to listen to how they were feeling, following the abuse. Finally, I would report the situation to my line manager so that he or she could determine whether further action should be taken or not.

NOTE: If you have previously been in this type of situation where you have witnessed someone being verbally abused, and taken positive action to stop it, tell the interview panel what you did and why using the STAR technique.

SAMPLE INTERVIEW QUESTION 5 TEMPLATE

Q. If you witnessed a member of your team at work being verbally abused, what would you do?

SAMPLE INTERVIEW QUESTION 6

Q. What is the code of ethics employed by this police force?

A. Whilst studying your website, I did come across the code of ethics you employ and I decided to learn it. Basically, when any police officer or member of staff feels the standards within the force have not been met they can report their concerns to the Ethics Committee. In addition to this, if any police officer or member of staff comes across a situation they feel unsure how to deal with, again they can raise this with the Ethics Committee. I would guess that the type of situation an officer might come across, whereby he or she were unsure how to deal with, would be if they attended a report of domestic abuse and a woman opened the door with a black eye. When the officer asks her what has happened, the woman says the child gave her the black eye by accident and then refuses to let them in. I would guess this type of situation would be potentially difficult to deal with and the Ethics Committee could assist and advise if situations such as this arose again in the future. From what I understand, officers and staff have the option to remain anonymous after reporting any incident or situation to the Ethics Committee, if they so wish.

SAMPLE INTERVIEW QUESTION 6 TEMPLATE

Q. What is the code of ethics employed by this police force?

SAMPLE INTERVIEW QUESTION 7

Q. What are the key priorities of this police force?

A. You currently have a large number of key priorities and these include cutting crime, catching criminals, dealing with anti-social behaviour, ensuring visible community policing is at the heart of everything you do, protecting the public from serious harm, providing a professional service by putting victims and witnesses first, meeting national commitments for policing, delivering value for money and also developing and supporting your workforce so they can do their job professionally and diligently.

NOTE: You should be able to find the key priorities for your chosen force on their website.

SAMPLE INTERVIEW QUESTION 7 TEMPLATE

Q. What are the key priorities of this police force?

SAMPLE INTERVIEW QUESTION 8

Q. We are interviewing forty people during the police officer final interviews, yet we only have vacancies for eighteen officers. What makes you better than the other applicants?

A. I believe I am the best candidate for this job for many reasons. First of all, I have been preparing for this role for many years now, by building up sufficient life experience and knowledge to be able to perform the role to a very high standard. Having studied all of the core competencies in detail, I feel I have plenty of experience to perform the duties of a police officer above and beyond the standards expected. I am a flexible person who will be available to work at all times, whether its day or night and also at weekends. I have a supportive family who fully understand, appreciate and support my dream of becoming a police officer with this police force. In addition to knowing my strengths, I am also aware of the areas I need to work on in order to improve, and I have been working on these to make sure I am fully prepared for the police training course, if successful. I have a good understanding and knowledge of the expectations that this police force expects from its staff, and I feel strongly that I will act as a good role model for the organisation that I am hoping to join. Finally, I understand that we live in times where the police force is under more scrutiny than ever and the requirement to be an employee who is open to and supportive of change has never been greater. Once again, I feel strongly that I can adapt to a constantly changing environment, and provide the exceptional service that the public expects from its police officers. I can assure you that, if you give me the opportunity, I will not let you down and I will work harder than anyone to excel in the role.

SAMPLE INTERVIEW QUESTION 8 TEMPLATE

Q. We are interviewing forty people during the police officer final interviews, yet we only have vacancies for eighteen officers. What makes you better than the other applicants?

SAMPLE INTERVIEW QUESTION 9

Q. Can you provide us with an example of a project you have recently successfully completed and and the obstacles you had to overcome?

A. Yes I can. I recently successfully completed a NEBOSH course (National Examination Board in Occupational Safety and Health) via distance learning. The course took two years to complete in total, and I had to carry out all studying in my own time, whilst holding down my current job as an Assistant Residential Building Site Manager. I decided to fund and undertake this qualification myself in order to further develop my knowledge and skills of my role, and to also improve my ability to perform my job to a high standard. The biggest obstacle I had to overcome was finding the time to complete the work to the high standard that I wanted to achieve. I decided to manage my time effectively and allocated two-hours every evening of the working week in which to complete the work required. Initially, I found the time management difficult; however, I stuck with it and was determined to complete the course successfully. In the end, I achieved good results, and I very much enjoyed the experience and challenge. I also feel that I drastically improved my time management and organisational skills as a result of undertaking this course. I have a determined nature, and I have the ability to concentrate for long periods of time when required, whilst organising and undertaking multiple tasks concurrently. I can be relied upon to finish projects to a high standard.

SAMPLE INTERVIEW QUESTION 9 TEMPLATE

Q. Can you provide us with an example of a project you have recently successfully completed and and the obstacles you had to overcome?

SAMPLE INTERVIEW QUESTION 10

Q. What are the standards of professional behaviour for this police force?

A. I did manage to locate and learn the standards of behaviour whilst studying your website. Whilst visiting my local police station to find out more about the role, the officer who showed me around and answered my questions, also mentioned how important these are. The standards are honesty and integrity, equality and diversity, use of force, authority, respect and courtesy, orders and instructions, duties and responsibilities, confidentiality, fitness for work, conduct and also challenging and reporting improper conduct. I understand these standards are very important to the role of a police officer, and I will ensure that I abide by them if successful.

SAMPLE INTERVIEW QUESTION 10 TEMPLATE

Q. What are the standards of professional behaviour for this police force?

SAMPLE INTERVIEW QUESTION 11

Q. What are the names of the stakeholders and agencies the police force work with on a local level?

A. The police force works with many different stakeholders and agencies, including:

Ambulance Service	Fire Service
Social Services	Local Authority
Local Housing Department	Police Commissioner
Health and Safety Executive	Air Accident Investigations Branch
British Transport Police	Crown Prosecution Service
Customs and Excise	CCTV operators
Department for Transport	Insurance Services
Driver and Vehicle Standards Agency	Independent Police Complaints Commission
Recovery and Breakdown operators	Samaritans
Victim Support	Office of Rail Regulation
Highways Agency	

NOTE: The above list is just a small example of the partner agencies and stakeholders that the police will work with. I recommend that you study the website of the police force you are applying to join, and also the Local Authority website, in order to learn more about the different agencies and stakeholders who work with the police on a local level.

SAMPLE INTERVIEW QUESTION 11 TEMPLATE

Q. What are the names of the stakeholders and agencies the police force work with on a local level?

SAMPLE INTERVIEW QUESTION 12

Q. What are the objectives of this police force with regards to equality?

A. During my research, I managed to find out that the current equality objectives of your force are to work towards increasing the number of black and minority ethnic officers, to match that of the population in the county area. In addition to this, you are taking positive steps towards retaining and developing black and minority ethnic colleagues into specialist and supervisory roles.

NOTE: Each police force will have their own objectives with regards to equality. Please make sure you study the website of the police force that you are applying to join, in order to study their own equality policy.

SAMPLE INTERVIEW QUESTION 12 TEMPLATE

Q. What are the objectives of this police force with regards to equality?

SAMPLE INTERVIEW QUESTION 13

Q. If a senior police officer told you to do something that you disagreed with, what would you do?

A. First and foremost I would obey his or her orders, as long as it was a lawful order. I understand I am joining a disciplined service, and it would be important that I followed their instructions.

Then, if after the incident or situation there was an opportunity for me to express my view in a respectful, positive and constructive manner, I would do so. I would always respect instructions and orders given to me, and perform any task to the highest possible standard.

SAMPLE INTERVIEW QUESTION 13 TEMPLATE

Q. If a senior police officer told you to do something that you disagreed with, what would you do?

SAMPLE INTERVIEW QUESTION 14

Q. What is ANPR and how are we using it within this county to reduce vehicle-related crime?

A. ANPR stands for Automatic Number Plate Recognition. When a vehicle passes a ANPR camera that is being monitored by the police, its registration number is read and instantly checked against database records. This enables the police to monitor and look out for vehicles of interest. This information and data allows police officers to intercept and stop a vehicle, check it for evidence and, where necessary, make arrests.

I understand that Automatic Number Plate Recognition has proved to be highly-effective in the detection of many offences, including locating stolen vehicles, tackling uninsured vehicle use and investigating cases of major crime.

It also allows officers' attention to be drawn to offending vehicles whilst allowing law abiding drivers to go about their business unhindered.

SAMPLE INTERVIEW QUESTION 14 TEMPLATE

Q. What is ANPR and how are we using it within this county to reduce vehicle-related crime?

SAMPLE INTERVIEW QUESTION 15

Q. Do you think the police force provide value for money to the public? If so, why?

A. Absolutely, one-hundred percent I believe the police force offers value for money. Whilst I very much want to become a police officer and work within the force, I too live in the local community and I have only seen great things from the police. From what I can see on a local level in my community, the police work very hard to educate the public and reduce crime, despite having limited resources. I understand that the police force budget has been reduced over recent years, yet despite this, your website shows that the force is becoming more efficient in tackling crime than ever before. For example, your force has managed to reduce vehicle related crime by seventeen percent over the last twelve months. I was very impressed by those statistics. I would imagine that, whilst the media and press can be very helpful in helping the police to catch offenders and reduce crime, sometimes the police can be painted in a negative light by them. On that basis, I would imagine it would be part of my job as a police officer to act as a positive role model for the police and work hard to educate the public about the good work the force is doing and demonstrate value for money is being delivered.

SAMPLE INTERVIEW QUESTION 15 TEMPLATE

Q. Do you think the police force provide value for money to the public? If so, why?

SAMPLE INTERVIEW QUESTION 16

Q. You are attending a local school talking to the children about the work of the police force. The teacher asks you to explain to the children how to call 999 in an emergency. What would you tell them?

A. I would tell them that they should only call 999 if it is an emergency. I would then give them examples of when to call 999, including if a crime is happening right now, someone is in immediate danger, there is a risk of serious damage to property, a suspect for a serious crime is nearby, or there is a traffic collision involving injury or danger to other road users. I would then use the opportunity to educate the children on why it is important they do not make hoax calls under any circumstances, as this could block the telephone lines for someone who really does need the police or other emergency services. I would then tell the children that the police do have an alternative number they can call if it is a non-emergency. The number they would need in a non-emergency situation is 101, and I would then give them additional examples of non-emergency situations, such as reporting a crime not currently in progress, giving information to the police about crime in their area, speaking to the police about a general enquiry and also contacting a specific police officer or member of staff. Finally, I would then ask the children if any of them had any questions to make sure they understood the information I had provided them with.

SAMPLE INTERVIEW QUESTION 16 TEMPLATE

Q. You are attending a local school talking to the children about the work of the police force. The teacher asks you to explain to the children how to call 999 in an emergency. What would you tell them?

SAMPLE INTERVIEW QUESTION 17

Q. Can you give an example of when you have challenged inappropriate behaviour in a working environment?

A. Yes, I can. I currently work as an IT consultant and I was carrying out contract work for a large corporate company in Manchester. I was having a tea break on my own in the company canteen, when I overheard a man calling one of his co-workers a "stupid old tart". I immediately went over to the man and said in a calm and respectful manner that I found his comment to be offensive, and requested that he didn't use that type of language, as it is unwelcome. I could sense he was angered by my comments, and he proceeded to tell me to mind my own business. I remained calm, and reiterated my request, by asking him once again not to use that type of offensive language in the workplace. I stated that, if he continued to use that type of language, I would report him to the company Managing Director. He immediately changed his tone, apologised and then got up and left the canteen. I then spoke to the lady whom the comment was directed at and explained the reasons why I had intervened. She told me she was grateful for my interaction and said that he often spoke to her in that manner. To my amazement, she informed me that the man who made the comment was in fact her line manager. After I left the canteen, I sent an email directly to the Managing Director of the company informing her of what I had just witnessed in the canteen, whilst also explaining what I had done to prevent it from happening again. I would never hesitate to challenge any type of behaviour that was either inappropriate, bullying in nature or discriminatory. This type of behaviour is not acceptable and should be challenged.

SAMPLE INTERVIEW QUESTION 17 TEMPLATE

Q. Can you give an example of when you have challenged inappropriate behaviour in a working environment?

SAMPLE INTERVIEW QUESTION 18

Q. You are a serving police officer and you are on foot patrol in the local town centre on a busy Friday night. The time is 11pm, and a member of public runs up to you and tells you that a fight has just started in the pub opposite. You look over to the pub and you can see the fight has already spilled out into the road. From what you can see, there appears to be a group of at least ten men fighting. Whilst I understand you are not a serving police officer, tell me what you think you would do in this type of situation?

A. To begin with, I would make sure that I followed my training and the operational procedures I would have learnt during my training course and tutoring. I would act fast, whilst remaining calm and in control and the safety of the public would be my number one priority. I would make a rapid assessment of the scene, before calling the control centre to request back up. I would make my way over to the scene whilst shouting out to the group of men that the police were now in attendance and they were to stop fighting. I would make my observations regarding which men were involved, including taking a mental note of what they looked like and what clothes they were wearing. I would tell everyone who was not involved in the fight to stay in the pub or stay a safe distance away from the scene. Then, if safe to do so, I would try to break up the fight and arrest any individuals involved. Once back up arrived, I would request that the attending officers assist with arresting further individuals involved in the fight, and also with taking statements from witnesses. Finally, once the scene was safe, I would speak to the manager of the pub to see if the CCTV had picked up the incident. The footage from any CCTV images captured would allow me to build a picture as to why the fight happened and also who was involved. At all times I would focus on safety, and also make sure that I followed my training and operational procedures.

SAMPLE INTERVIEW QUESTION 18 TEMPLATE

Q. You are a serving police officer and you are on foot patrol in the local town centre on a busy Friday night. The time is 11pm, and a member of public runs up to you and tells you that a fight has just started in the pub opposite. You look over to the pub and you can see the fight has already spilled out into the road. From what you can see, there appears to be a group of at least ten men fighting. Whilst I understand you are not a serving police officer, tell me what you think you would do in this type of situation?

SAMPLE INTERVIEW QUESTION 19

Q. Police officers are required to work closely with others in order to complete difficult and pressurised tasks. Can you give me an example of when you have worked closely as part of a team to achieve a goal?

A. Yes, I have a number of examples that I can draw upon that demonstrate my ability to work as part of a team. One in particular is where I recently volunteered to work with three new members of our team at work. The task required us all to successfully complete a stock-take of the entire warehouse, within a 60-minute timeframe. Our warehouse is huge, and we hold over one thousand different lines of product. The reason why the stock-take had to be completed quickly was due to the fact that a large number of items had gone missing, and the Warehouse Manager needed to compile a report for the Area Manager, who was on his way down from Manchester. Allegedly, one of the delivery drivers had been taking stock without permission and then selling it on for his own personal gain. The reason why I volunteered for the task is because I am a conscientious person, who enjoys working with other people and who also enjoys working under pressure where a definitive timescale is involved. I quickly gathered the other team members together and explained how urgent the task was. I then showed the other team members how to stock-take properly by focusing initially on just one aisle. Once they had learnt the stock-taking process, and they had confirmed to me they all understood, we worked together in a methodical manner working down one aisle at a time. Periodically I would stop to ensure that the task was being done correctly, and to also establish whether or not the other team members needed assistance with any element of the stock-taking task. At the end of the specified timeframe we had completed the stock-take, and were able to provide accurate figures to the Warehouse Manager who in turn managed to prepare his report for the Area Manager. Whilst working as a team member I always concentrate on effective communication, focusing on the task in hand and also providing support to team members who require assistance. I fully understand how important it is to work as part of a team within the police force and I can be relied upon to be a competent team member at all times.

SAMPLE INTERVIEW QUESTION 19 TEMPLATE

Q. Police officers are required to work closely with others in order to complete difficult and pressurised tasks. Can you give me an example of when you have worked closely as part of a team to achieve a goal?

SAMPLE INTERVIEW QUESTION 20

Q. What type of work do you think you will be undertaking as a police officer, if you are successful?

A. I believe the work I would undertake will be extremely diverse and varied in nature, and that the role would require me to use a wide remit of skills and expertise. To begin with, I would be acting as a positive role model for the police force, by behaving with honesty and integrity; and delivering a service to the public that exceeds their expectations. I would also be providing, on a daily basis, a reassuring high-visibility presence within the community, whilst also responding to incidents, gathering evidence and taking contemporaneous notes and statements of incidents and reports of crimes as and when they are reported. I would be required to attend and protect crime scenes, and also investigate incidents through effective policing and by also following my training and operational procedures at all times. I would make arrests when appropriate, complete custody procedures and also interview suspects and present evidence in court. I would liaise and work with other stakeholders and agencies, to make sure that we all worked towards the common goal of protecting the community in which we serve. I would also be required to put vulnerable people, victims of crime and witnesses first. I would be required to face challenging and difficult situations on a daily basis, and I would need to be at my best at all times to ensure I uphold the principles of policing. Finally, I would be required to adopt the core competencies of the police officer's role, and utilise interpersonal skills to diffuse and respond with integrity in any situation.

SAMPLE INTERVIEW QUESTION 20 TEMPLATE

Q. What type of work do you think you will be undertaking as a police officer, if you are successful?

SAMPLE INTERVIEW QUESTION 21

Q. Can you give an example of when you have been resilient and taken the responsibility to communicate an important message to a group of people?

A. Yes, I certainly can. Whilst working in my current position as a retail sales assistant I was the duty manager for the day as my manager had called in sick. It was the week before Christmas, and the shop was very busy. During the day, the fire alarm went off, and I started to ask everybody to evacuate the shop, which is our company policy. The alarm has gone off in the past, but the normal manager usually lets people stay in the shop whilst he finds out if it's a false alarm. This was a difficult situation because the shop was very busy, nobody wanted to leave, and my shop assistants were disagreeing with me in my decision to evacuate the shop. Some of the customers were becoming irate, as they were in the changing rooms at the time. Both the customers and my shop assistants were disagreeing with me. The customers were saying that it was appalling that they had to evacuate the shop and that they would complain to the Head Office about it. My sales staff were also trying to persuade me to keep everybody inside the shop and that it was most probably a false alarm, like it usually is. I was determined to evacuate everybody from the shop for safety reasons and would not allow anybody to deter me from my aim. The safety of my staff and customers was at the forefront of my mind, even though it wasn't at theirs. I persisted with my actions by remaining calm, resilient and confident. I relayed my instructions for everyone to evacuate the shop again with a firm voice and finally everybody stated to leave the shop. When the Fire Service arrived they informed me that there had been a small fire at the rear of the shop and that the actions I had taken were correct. Everybody was safe and nobody was hurt as a result of the incident. I am a resilient and confident person and would never be swayed by someone else's opinion if I felt their safety was in danger.

SAMPLE INTERVIEW QUESTION 21 TEMPLATE

Q. Can you give an example of when you have been resilient and taken the responsibility to communicate an important message to a group of people?

SAMPLE INTERVIEW QUESTION 22

Q. Can you give an example of when you have supported diversity in the workplace?

A. I currently work as an office administrator for a small architect design business in London. We have an open plan office and there are 27 staff in total. It's a busy and friendly office, and we are always taking on new staff to cope with our expansion plans. Last month, a new member of the team joined. She was going to be working as an admin assistant, just like me, and I was keen to help her settle in and show her the ropes. When she arrived, she came into the office in a wheelchair. I introduced myself to her straight away, made her feel welcome and said that I would show her to her new work station. As we made our way over to her desk, which was at the other end of the office, I suddenly realised that she would potentially have problems making her way to the toilets and also the kitchen area. Whilst our office building is equipped to accommodate people in wheelchairs, I felt the desk we had provided her with was not really in the best location. I decided to make a suggestion to her. Basically, my desk is located not too far away from both the toilet facilities and also the kitchen area, and I told her that I was going to swap desks with her to make her life a bit easier in the office. She told me that I didn't need to do that, but I insisted. I told her that we were a very welcoming office and any other member of staff would also do the same. I then took the lady back over to my office space and started to move my things over to where her desk was located. It only took me twenty minutes to move all of my things to the new desk and I could sense the lady was pleased that I insisted on moving her to the better location. A few other members of the office team saw what I was doing, and they joined in by helping me move my things to the new desk. This small act had a big impact on helping the new member of staff to settle in. Not only did she feel more valued and appreciated, but it also helped to make her recognise that we, as a company, support diversity and do all we can to ensure every member of staff feels welcome, valued and appreciated.

SAMPLE INTERVIEW QUESTION 22 TEMPLATE

Q. Can you give an example of when you have supported diversity in the workplace?

SAMPLE INTERVIEW QUESTION 23

Q. How can we, as a local police force, improve relations with the local community?

A. I think there are a number of different ways you can improve relations. I am sure you do many of these things already, but promoting all of the good work you do within the community via the local press will help to demonstrate to the public that the good work you are doing is making a difference to their lives. I also feel that working closely with community groups and community leaders can be a positive thing, to demonstrate that the police force is listening to people's concerns and issues. I also think that it is very important that the police follow up and keep people updated with progress on policing matters. For example, if the police hold community meetings where local residents are encouraged to share their concerns, somebody must follow up with a progress report or communicate what work has been done to deal with their concerns, if they are a policing-related matter. I would also imagine that it is my responsibility as a police officer, if I am to be successful, to be as visible as possible within the community. It would be my job to speak to people and reassure them that the police are there to serve them and provide a reassuring presence. I also feel that relations with the police has to start at an early age. I understand budgets must be very restricted, but if police officers are able to attend schools and talk to children from an early age about the type of work they do, that can only be a good thing and it will help to give the children a positive impression of the police from an early age. Community policing, I would imagine, means working proactively and building relationships in the face of tension and issues. So, if there are problems within a particular area that I am serving in, it would be my job to help ease those tensions and build better relationships with the community by working alongside community leaders. I guess the police service would cease to function without the active support of the communities it serves. Effective community engagement, targeted foot patrols and collaborative problem solving would significantly increase public confidence in policing activity.

SAMPLE INTERVIEW QUESTION 23 TEMPLATE

Q. How can we, as a local police force, improve relations with the local community?

SAMPLE INTERVIEW QUESTION 24

Q. How do you keep yourself physically fit?

A. I take personal responsibility for my fitness and I fully understand how important this would be to my role as a police officer. At present, I go running four times a week in the mornings before I start work. I like to get up early and get my fitness routine out of the way, which then leaves me time to spend with my family once I get home from work. I usually run five kilometers each time, and this ensures my body fat is kept to a healthy level and my concentration levels are at their peak. My current job involves me having to concentrate for long periods of time and I have a responsibility to make sure I can perform at work to a high standard. At weekends, I spend time playing hockey for a local team. We are not overly competitive; however, I like the fact I get to play a team sport and interact with other people from the community. We also go out together socially once a month and I really enjoy that side of being part of a hockey team.

SAMPLE INTERVIEW QUESTION 24 TEMPLATE

Q. How do you keep yourself physically fit?

SAMPLE INTERVIEW QUESTION 25

Q. Why do you think the police force is keen to recruit more people from black and ethnic minority groups (BME) and do you have any suggestions for how we might achieve that aim?

A. If the police force is to deliver a consistently high level of service, then it needs to be representative of the community that it serves. Our community is diverse in nature; therefore, so should the police force be, if it is to achieve its aims and goals. The police could offer introductory programmes or courses to people who are looking to join the service from under-represented groups. These courses could aim to show people what it is like to work within the police service and also give them tours of police stations, the training centre and also give them the opportunity to speak to already serving police officers from black and ethnic minority backgrounds. People could also have a try at the police fitness test, to see if they have what it takes to pass. This type of introductory course or programme would give people the opportunity to learn more about the service, before they commit to applying. Conversely, it would also give the police the opportunity to find out why so few people from under-represented groups actually apply. This type of information might be invaluable to the police as there might be specific reasons why not enough people are joining. I would imagine that many people consider applying to become a police officer but think it's not for them for a variety of reasons, such as not having the right levels of fitness or fear their decision won't be supported by family and friends. During this type of introductory course or programme, potential applicants could also take along with them their family and friends, which would in turn give them the support they need during their application to the police.

SAMPLE INTERVIEW QUESTION 25 TEMPLATE

Q. Why do you think the police force is keen to recruit more people from black and ethnic minority groups (BME) and do you have any suggestions for how we might achieve that aim?

SAMPLE INTERVIEW QUESTION 26

Q. What is the structure of this police force?

A. During my research, I found out that the police service in Kent is comprised of three divisions: north, east and west. Each division is headed up by a Divisional Commander, whose rank is Chief Superintendent. Under each divisional commander are various districts, which in turn are headed up by a Chief Inspector. East division consists of various districts which include Ashford and Shepway, Canterbury and Dover, and finally Thanet. North division includes Gravesham and Dartford and also Medway and Swale. West division includes Maidstone, Sevenoaks, Tonbridge and Tunbridge Wells.

NOTE: The above sample response is for the county police service of Kent. You should be able to find the structure of your local police service on their website. My advice is to also <u>consider</u> learning, (time permitting) the names of each police station for each division/district and also the names of the Chief Superintendent and Chief Inspector for each division/district. You should also learn the names and ranks of the senior management team for your chosen police service and also the name of the Police and Crime Commissioner.

SAMPLE INTERVIEW QUESTION 26 TEMPLATE

Q. What is the structure of this police force?

SAMPLE INTERVIEW QUESTION 27

Q. Tell me the different stages of police officer training and probation you will go through and which areas, if any, you will find the hardest?

A. The Initial Police Learning and Development Programme (IPLDP) will last for 10 weeks. During this initial stage, I will be taught a number of legislative and practical skills. This part of training also includes operationally based and assessed role plays, an interview skills course and opportunities to work in the community as well as a number of lessons from experienced officers from the county in areas that will be relevant to my role as a police constable. After that stage of the process, providing I have passed, I will commence onto the community placements stage. During this stage, which lasts for 3 days, I will learn to improve my knowledge and understanding of the county area and its needs; improve my policing skills in relation to diverse communities and also learn how to promote trust and understanding between the police and hard to reach and hard to hear communities. Then, once I have successfully completed the community placements stage, I would move on to the tutoring stage of the process. This would only happen if my trainers are satisfied that I have adequately passed the IPLDP and the community placements stage. I understand that, as part of the tutoring unit, I would get to develop my skills further in an operational environment. I would work either on a 1-1 or 1-2 basis, dealing with day-to-day incidents on response teams, whilst also having an opportunity to work with local neighbourhood teams, and also to carry out interviews and low level investigations. Once my tutor constable is satisfied with my performance and progress, I would move on to the independent patrol status. Once independent patrol status is achieved, I understand that I will be then be asked to complete a Level 3 Diploma in Policing. This is designed to provide evidence that I have the skills necessary to perform at an acceptable standard as a police officer. This period would last up to two years, during which time I will be supported by a police officer assessor. I will have regular meetings with him or her, during which time I will need to evidence my achievements, in order that the assessor can identify which areas I need to focus attention on to develop my skills.

With regards to the elements of the training and probationary period I would find the hardest, I believe I could find learning new skills the toughest. Until recently, I have been out of the educational environment for ten years. However, in my preparation for joining the police force, I decided to embark on an *Introduction to Law* course at my local college. The lessons take place in the evening, and this has given me the chance to learn new skills, whilst also placing myself under pressure, as I have been required to carry out homework and undertake exams. To be honest, I have found the experience to be highly enjoyable and rewarding. I am now confident that I will be able to take on all of the new skills I need to learn, if I am successful in my pursuit in my application to becoming a police officer.

NOTE: The above example should not be used for your own response. Please make sure you study your own police force's initial training programme and probationary period in order to structure your own response to this question.

SAMPLE INTERVIEW QUESTION 27 TEMPLATE

Q. Tell me the different stages of police officer training and probation you will go through and which areas, if any, you will find the hardest?

SAMPLE INTERVIEW QUESTION 28

Q. Can you tell me about a time when you have promoted and supported change in an organisation?

A. Yes, I can. I currently work as a care assistant for the Local Authority. Just a few months ago, all of the care workers were called into a meeting by the Area Manager. We all sat down in the meeting, and the Area Manager began to explain how a number of potentially disruptive changes to our working practices were coming into force very soon. The changes were required in order for our department to meet its care quality standards targets. I could sense that a number of people within the room were unhappy with the suggestion of change and they began to make their feelings known to the manager. I put my hand up to speak, and made a suggestion to everyone in the room that we should give our manager the respect she deserves and allow her to at least finish explaining what the changes were and how they would impact on our working lives, before voicing our own opinions. Everyone then agreed to remain silent until the manager had finished her talk. The manager went on to explain that everyone would be affected within the department and, in particular, our shift patterns would alter, but that our total working hours would stay the same. She went on further to explain that we would all have the opportunity to work extra hours, at double-pay, if we wanted to. At the end of her talk, some of the care workers were still clearly upset and angered by the pending changes. After they had had the opportunity to express their feelings, I stated my own opinion to the group. I explained that we all now work in an ever-changing environment, and we would all need to adapt to change, as the change would only increase as the years went on. I also explained that change could actually be a positive thing if we all embraced it, and at the very least, we should all give it a try. Some people in the room seemed surprised at my positive attitude, and I think they expected me to be more "on their side", whilst they were challenging our Area Manager. One thing is for sure, I was not going to allow the negative talk some people were engaging in, affect my own working life. At the end of the meeting, everyone agreed to at least try and embrace the changes to see how much they affected our working lives. We also all agreed to all meet up again in three months' time with our Area Manager, in order to discuss the changes and how we were getting on. I believe that my positive attitude and contributions during the meeting allowed the team to at least try to embrace the new changes that were coming into force.

SAMPLE INTERVIEW QUESTION 28 TEMPLATE

Q. Can you tell me about a time when you have promoted and supported change in an organisation?

SAMPLE INTERVIEW QUESTION 29

Q. What issues are affecting this police force at present?

A. During my research, I was studying both your website and other useful online resources, to find out the types of issues impacting the police both locally and nationally. From what I understand, the police service is facing a number of challenges that will require highly effective leadership and the ability of police officers to adapt and change their working practices. For example, there has been a huge increase in cyber-related crime and incidents which need to be investigated. These, understandably, take up a huge amount of time and resources and can often be very difficult to investigate. In addition to cyber-related crime, the opportunities for people to actually report crime are far better than they used to be. Whilst this is very much a positive thing, collecting and using data and information relating to reported crimes and incidents can take time and resources. The police service has a huge challenge ahead of them in order to stay on top of reported crime and to also investigate incidents thoroughly. I would also imagine there is a challenge for the police service in respect of which types of reported crime to prioritise, based on the limited resources it has at its disposal. Once again, police officers would need to be highly-efficient in their work, to help the service achieve its goals and targets. Another issue affecting the police service will be the recruitment of under-represented groups and BME officers. The police service needs to be representative of the communities in which it serves, if it is to continually provide the exceptional levels of service it currently provides. From my research and studies, I also understand there are challenges for the police service with regards to breaking the repeat offender cycle. Only by working with other agencies and stakeholders can the police service collate sufficient data and information to look at new ways to prevent people from reoffending. Whilst I am sure there are many other issues and challenges affecting the police service both locally and nationally, these were the ones that appeared prominent whist carrying out my research and studies.

SAMPLE INTERVIEW QUESTION 29 TEMPLATE

What issues are affecting this police force at present?

SAMPLE INTERVIEW QUESTION 30

Q. Can you tell me about a time when you have gathered information from a wide range of sources before making a difficult decision?

A. Actually, I was involved in a situation of this nature quite recently. Whilst at work it came to my attention that a colleague was not pulling his weight. In addition to not doing his job properly, there had been a couple of times whereby I could smell alcohol on his breath. I was naturally concerned for his welfare and also concerned for the fact that other team members were starting to get frustrated with his lack of performance within the team. Our line manager was away on holiday for two weeks, so I decided to see if I could do anything to stop this situation from deteriorating any further. I also wanted to see if I could resolve this issue before my line manager returned to work. Whilst I would still need to report my concerns to my line manager when she got back, I wanted to do all I could to get to the bottom of this, as it was starting to affect the team. I thought carefully about the actions that I was going to take, and decided that the best course of action would be to gather as much information as possible from a variety of sources. Before speaking to my colleague about his work issues and the smell of alcohol, I wanted to ask my other colleagues within the team whether any of them were aware that our colleague was having problems at home. It's sometimes far too easy to jump into a situation, and start accusing someone of wrongdoing without first of all gathering the facts. After speaking to members of my team, it became apparent that our colleague was suffering from depression. Apparently, his girlfriend of eight years had run off with his friend, and he was finding things very difficult to deal with. This, in turn, was starting to have a negative impact on his personal and working life and he was allegedly turning to alcohol in order to drown his sorrows. Because of the seriousness of the situation, I then decided to speak to our Human Resources department before sitting down with my work colleague to see what types of support were available for people in his situation. As it transpires, our organisation offers free counselling for people who need it, but the referral would need to come from our line manager first. At this stage I felt I had sufficient background information to speak to our work colleague who was underperforming. I think that, without carrying out my research and gathering the background information that I now had, I could have quite easily made the situation worse by criticising our colleague because of his under-performance at work and the smell of alcohol on his breath. With the information I had, I would now take an entirely different approach when speaking to him. I asked my colleague to come and sit with me during tea break in quiet room where we would not be disturbed. I explained to him that I was genuinely worried for him and that I wanted to help him out. I asked him if he wanted to talk to me about anything at all and I reassured him that whatever he told me would be treated with confidence. Before he could even say anything, his eyes filled up and he started to cry. I put my arms around him and told him not to worry and that everything would be fine. After a short while, he started to talk and told me about the situation he was in with regards to his girlfriend of eight years running off with his friend. He went on to explain that he was drinking heavily at night to get over the pain. I listened to him carefully and then decided to take control of the situation by making some positive suggestions that were designed to help him. I asked for his permission to speak to our line manager so that we could get him some help through the counselling service the organisation offered. Thankfully, he agreed to give this a try. I told him that, as soon as our line manager returned to work, I would ask her to start the referral process for getting him some much-needed counselling. Finally, I gave him my mobile telephone number and said that we should speak every day until our line manager returned to work. I explained how I would be there to support him through this difficult time and that I would be there to listen at any time, day or night. Whilst this situation was very difficult to deal with, especially due to its sensitive nature, I felt that by gathering all of the facts first it gave me the opportunity to make the right decisions and ultimately take the right course of action.

SAMPLE INTERVIEW QUESTION 30 TEMPLATE

Q. Can you tell me about a time when you have gathered information from a wide range of sources before making a difficult decision?

FURTHER FINAL INTERVIEW QUESTIONS TO PREPARE FOR

Q. Are you an organised person? If you are, give me an example of when you have been highly organised in a work environment.

Q. What are the different ranks of the uniformed police service?

Q. Can you give an example of when you have made a difficult decision whilst working under pressure?

Probing question 1: What difficulties did you face whilst working under pressure?

Probing question 2: Would you do anything different if the same 'working under pressure' situation arose again?

Q. Can you tell me about a time when you have worked in partnership with others to solve a problem?

Q. Which parts of the police officer job do you think you'll like the most?

Q. Which parts of the police officer job do you think you'll dislike the most?

Q. Can you tell me about a time when you have had to defuse a conflict situation?

Q. Can you give me an example of when you have delivered outstanding customer service?

Q. Have you discussed your application to the police force with your friends and do you have the support of your family?

Q. Can you give an example of when you have demonstrated flexibility in the workplace?

Q. If you are unsuccessful at this attempt, what would you do?

Don't forget, the interview questions and sample responses that I have provided are not guaranteed to be the exact questions you will get asked during your interview. However, they will be a great basis on which to start your preparation. In addition to using this guide, please do make sure you carry out your own research both online and offline, and try to come up with your own anticipated interview questions prior to your interview.

A few final words

A FEW FINAL WORDS

So, we have now reached the final section of the guide and it is almost time for me to let you get on with your own preparation for the police officer interview. But, before I go, I wanted to give you a few final words of wisdom and motivational tips that will hopefully inspire you to achieving the highest scores possible at your interview. The fact that you have invested in this guide tells me one thing: you are *very* serious about passing the police officer final interview, and that can only be a good thing. It does not matter how much time you have left to prepare for your interview, just make sure you give it your all and make sure you leave the interview with no regrets.

Having personally worked in the emergency service for almost 17 years, I have nothing but praise for the great work the men and women of the UK police force do and the job of a police officer comes highly recommended. On that basis, the job is certainly worth fighting for and it is essential that you spend as much time as possible on your research and preparation. At the start of this guide I stated that success is in *your* hands and nobody else's, and I still maintain that is a fact. How much effort you put into this is down to you. Whether or not you carry out a mock interview (or preferably three or four!) is down to you. Whether or not you work on your communication skills and interview technique is down to you, and whether or not you prepare responses to every single questions contained within this guide is also down to you.

I wish you all the very best in your pursuit to becoming a police officer and please do get in touch via our website **www.How2Become.com** to let me know how you get on.

To your success,

Richard McMunn

ACE THE POLICE OFFICER SELECTION PROCESS!

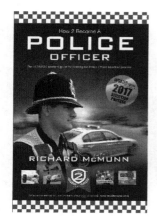

How2Become have created these FANTASTIC guides to assist you during the police officer selection process. Our products range from the initial application form, police tests, all the way up to the final interview. We also offer a 1 day course to help you prepare for each stage of the application process.

FOR MORE INFORMATION ON HOW TO BECOME A POLICE OFFICER, PLEASE CHECK OUT THE FOLLOWING:

WWW.HOW2BECOME.COM

****

Need further help preparing for your final interview?

Attend a one-to-one training session and mock final interview with a former MET police recruitment trainer in Kings Hill, Kent.

Skype sessions also available.

To find out more, or to secure your training, contact the How2Become team today at: info@How2Become.co.uk

****

Get Access To

FREE

Psychometric

Tests

www.MyPsychometricTests.co.uk